EMPTY!

CAN SOMETHING EMPTY EVER BE GOOD?

WRITTEN BY
JOSHUA COOLEY

ILLUSTRATED BY
JAMES ELSTON

10

Let's face it: Some things in life should never be **EMPTY**. Take, for instance, a cookie jar.

A cookie jar with no cookies in it? Why, that's enough to bring a tear to the eye!

Want to know what else
should never be **EMPTY?**

Your piggy bank.

A piggy bank with
nothing inside?
More tears!

Or imagine if you walked into your bedroom one day and noticed your pet hamster's cage was **EMPTY**.

Oh no!
Fuzzball
must have
escaped!
Where are you,
Fuzzball? Please
come home!

While we're on the subject, here are some other things that should never be **EMPTY** ...

Your stomach

Rumble, rumble ...

A party piñata

Big birthday blooper!

A swimming pool

Uh-oh. This is gonna hurt ...

Come to think of it, these things should never be **EMPTY** either ...

An ice cream carton

Argh! Who left this in the freezer?!

Shelves at the toy shop

No toys? Call the police! Send in the army!

It's a code-red emergency!

Christmas presents
That's just plain wrong.

HAPPY BIRTHDAY
A birthday party
happy birthday
This certainly isn't what I had in mind.

Your parachute
Gulp.

Yes, **EMPTY** can be bad. In fact, a long time ago, the entire universe was **EMPTY**. The Bible says that in the beginning, 'the earth was formless and **EMPTY**, and darkness covered the deep waters' (Genesis 1:2).

A big, dark, **EMPTY** world sounds pretty boring – and a little scary!

Well, God didn't want a big, dark, **EMPTY**, boring, and scary world. So he created a beautiful world filled with things for us to enjoy!

And yet, in God's big, beautiful world, **EMPTY** isn't always bad. Sometimes **EMPTY** can be very good! These things are wonderful when they're **EMPTY** ...

Amusement parks
No crowds!
No long queues!
ENTER
Oh, happy day!

That beehive you just bumped into
Phew! That was a close call.

But of all the wonderfully **EMPTY** things in the world, there's one that's *better* than all the rest. In fact, this **EMPTY** thing's emptiness is so fantabulously **EMPTY**, it can change your life forever!

Do you want to know what it is?

Do you *REALLY* want to know what it is?

IT'S JESUS'
EMPTY TOMB!

Jesus is the eternal Son of God. He is perfect in every way.

When he lived on earth, he taught God's truth and did many amazing things.

Then Jesus died on a cross for you and me. He did this because we needed someone *without* sin to save us from ours.

We've all disobeyed God. Without Jesus, our hearts are **EMPTY** of goodness and filled with sin. But out of his great love for us, Jesus died to take the punishment we deserve!

After Jesus died, his body was buried in a tomb. But Jesus didn't stay there. Remember, his tomb is ...

EMPTY!

Three days after Jesus died, he rose to life again. He's alive.

Jesus' **EMPTY** tomb is the greatest ***EMPTY*** in history!

What does Jesus' **EMPTY** tomb mean for you? It means ...

Jesus defeated sin and death!

Jesus loves you and wants you to follow him!

You can live forever with Jesus by trusting in him as your Lord and Saviour!

So whenever you're
sad about an
EMPTY fridge ...

or an **EMPTY**
toy box ...

or your
EMPTY
lunchbox
at school ...

Just remember
the best **EMPTY**
ever! You can
be forgiven
and live
forever with
Jesus all
because ...

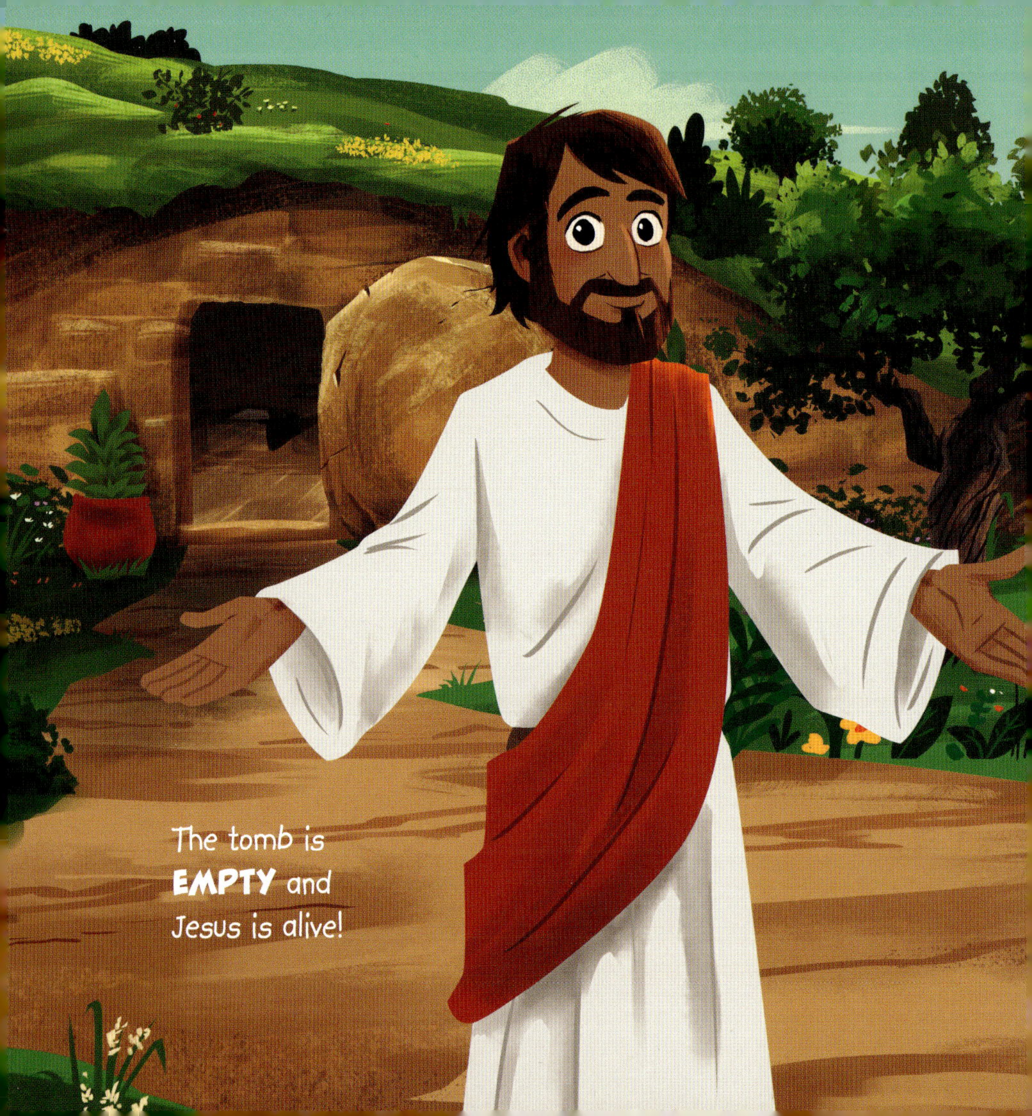

The tomb is
EMPTY and
Jesus is alive!

'I am the living one. I died, but look – I am alive forever and ever!'

REVELATION 1:18

JOSHUA COOLEY is a *New York Times* bestselling author who has written a variety of books, including *I Can't Believe My Eyes*. He lives in Durham, North Carolina. You can visit his website at www.joshuacooleyauthor.com.

JAMES ELSTON is a Nashville-based illustrator who started his career as an animation artist for Disney before working on a variety of projects including *VeggieTales* and, recently, *The Wingfeather Saga* TV series.

To every child who has felt an emptiness inside. There is a risen, living **SAVIOUR** who can fill you with eternal love, hope, and joy!

Empty! Anglicised Text © 2025 Joshua Cooley. Illustrations © 2025 James Elston.

All rights reserved. Except as may be permitted by the Copyright Act, no part of this publication may be reproduced in any form or by any means without prior permission from the publisher.

Scripture quotations are taken from the Holy Bible, New Living Translation, copyright ©1996, 2004, 2015 by Tyndale House Foundation. Used by permission of Tyndale House Publishers, Carol Stream, Illinois 60188. All rights reserved.

Paperback ISBN: 9781837280315
Hardback ISBN: 9781837280469

Published by 10Publishing, a division of 10ofThose Ltd.,
Tomlinson Road, Leyland, Lancs, PR25 2DY, England.
info@10ofthose.com | www.10ofthose.com

Written by Joshua Cooley, Illustrated by James Elston
Designed by Pete Barnsley

1 3 5 7 10 8 6 4 2